LeANN
RIMES

LeANN RIMES

by **Mark Bego**

ST. MARTIN'S GRIFFIN

NEW YORK

In memory of "Grandma" Catherine Bego

Design by Pop Culture

Picture credits: RETNA PICTURES LIMITED (P.7&11 Steve Granitz, P.17&27 Daniel Peebles, P.24&69 Chris Craft, P.59 Bill Davilla), STARFILE (P.8 Mike Guastella, P.13/22/53&66 Jeffrey Mayer, P.35&43 Mark Harlan, P.36/54&73 Chuck Palin, P.41 Robert Hernandez, P.47 Dominick Conde, P.56 Gene Shaw), TAMMIE ARROYO (P.14/18/21/29/31/33/39/44/48/60/63/65/71/74/79), ROGER SEALY (P.51&top of 77), BOBBIE ANN STIMAC (bottom of P.77)
Cover Picture: RETNA PICTURES LIMITED

ISBN   0-312-19378-5

First St. Martin's Griffin Edition: October 1998

ACKNOWLEDGEMENTS

The author would like to thank the following people for their help on this book, and/or their assistance in gathering information on LeAnn Rimes:

• Marie Morreale (Mutha, you're wonderful!)
• A.J. Flick of the "Tucson Citizen" and Susan Mittelkauf (Glad we three got to see LeAnn together!!!)
• Carolyn Howe of the "National Enquirer" (Inquiring minds DO want to know!)
• Glenn Hughes (for taping the LeAnn performances on TV!)
• Victoria Green Elliott (Thanks for the info, and for my seating assignment!)
• Virginia Lohle (You are a fabulous friend, thanks for thinking of me when this book came along)
• Zi Siddique of Power Publishing in London
• Jim Fitzgerald of St. Martin's Press (We finally got to work together!...now buy my novel!!!)
• Mary Wilson (...just for being so Supreme!!!)

Special Thanks to my NYC Innkeepers:

• The glamorous Marcy MacDonald
• The stunning Sindi Markoff
• The dazzling Ann Watt
• The ever-wonderful Glenn Hughes

CONTENTS

RHYTHM AND RIMES

With reference to the purity of youth, the old saying goes: "From out of the mouths of babes, comes the truth." Well, if the child in question is the startlingly talented 15-year-old Ms. LeAnn Rimes, not only does the truth come out of her mouth, but also, rhythm, country, soul, heartbreaking ballads, and the blues.

As the youngest, most talented and biggest-selling new artist of the late 1990's, LeAnn Rimes has literally taken Nashville, and all of America by storm. Debuting with her dynamic single, "Blue" in 1996, this gifted young superstar is racking up honors and accolades quicker than anyone in the business. Tallying both albums and singles, in the first two years since she exploded onto the national and international scene, she has sold well over 14 million copies of her recordings.

Her debut album, "Blue" very quickly hit Number One on both the Country and Pop music charts, and to date has sold over 5 million copies in the United States alone. (V) Her second album release, "Unchained Melody / The Early Years," also hit the top of the charts, and is certified "Double Platinum" for sales of over two million copies. And, catching up with those impressive track records, her latest two-million-selling "Double Platinum" LP, "You Light Up My Life / Inspirational Songs" debuted at Number One on three separate charts: Country, Pop, and Contemporary Christian. She is the very first artist of any sort to accomplish that impressive task. In an industry where the bottom line lies in the sales figures one amasses, LeAnn Rimes is a qualified "smash!" As of the beginning of 1998, LeAnn has sold over eight million copies of her appealing, and exciting albums, and this is just the start!

As beloved as she is by the record-buying public, LeAnn Rimes has also gotten the unanimous support of the music industry. In October of 1996 she became the youngest artist ever to win the prestigious Horizon Award from the Country Music Association. In February of 1997 she became not only the youngest artist ever to win the "Best New Artist" Grammy Award, but she is also the only country performer to be awarded that trophy.

To magnify the stakes even farther, LeAnn won, not one, but two 1997 Grammy Awards that New York City winter's night: in the categories of "Best Female Country Vocal Performance" for the song "Blue," in addition to the coveted "Best New Artist" trophy. The latter award was an even more special honor, in that Rimes was the first country artist to even be nominated in that category since Bobbie ("Ode To Billy Joe") Gentry in 1967. Unlike Gentry, she walked away with the award, held tightly in her hands. Anyone who witnessed LeAnn's exciting and tearful acceptance speech, broadcast live from New York City's famed Madison Square Garden, will attest to the glory of that moment. It was a brilliant honor

for country music, and for LeAnn Rimes. According to the teenaged superstar, "The Grammy—that was a blast! I was the second country artist ever to be nominated [in that category], and the only one to ever win it. I think it was a shock to everyone." (A)

In the spring of 1997, LeAnn won three awards at the Academy of Country Music Awards. LeAnn won for Top New Female Vocalist, and her recording of "Blue" won trophies in the categories of Top Single and Top Song Of The Year. And in December of 1997, she was named the "Entertainer Of The Year" by the Billboard Music Awards, and won three additional trophies.

Not only is LeAnn a phenomenally successful singer, but she has already been expanding her own creative horizons into other artistic fields. She has mastered songwriting, and has released two of her own compositions—"Talk To Me" and "Share My Love"—on her albums. Her first book, "Holiday In Your Heart" (written with Tom Carter) was a big hit when it was published in the fall of 1997. In fact, it was so popular that it was immediately turned into a screenplay, and became the vehicle for her first filmed acting performance. The made-for-TV movie, "Holiday In Your Heart" was a huge ratings success when it debuted on ABC-TV on December 14, 1997. She proved to be a very natural actress, even while appearing opposite a respected Broadway and screen legend like Bernadette Peters.

"Holiday In Your Heart," was in fact so successful, both critically and in the TV ratings, that it is certain to become a perennial Christmas season film, and it is predicted to stand the test of time. It will undoubtedly become remembered warmly as the kind of milestone in LeAnn's career, that "The Wizard Of Oz" is looked upon as part of the legend of Judy Garland. For LeAnn Rimes, this is only the beginning.

It is as though every other decade, a dynamic country female singer in her teens shows up on the record charts and makes everyone in earshot stand up and notice—in a big way. In the 1950's it was diminutive Brenda Lee, and her string of scorching hits like "Sweet Nothin's." In the 1970's it was brassy Tanya Tucker, and her sizzling debut with "Delta Dawn." Well, in the 1990's, the brass ring has been seized by none other than LeAnn Rimes, and the showstopping power ballad, "Blue," which launched her career at the top of the charts.

Even more astounding than the fact that she was fourteen when she recorded and released the hit version of the song "Blue," is the determination and drive that this young girl has had all of her life. She made her first public performance at the age of two, and recorded the album "Unchained Melody / The Early Years" when she was only eleven!

LeAnn is the biggest and most successful young hit maker since pop star Debbie Gibson had her "Platinum" streak of hits in the 1980's. Gibson has since gone on to become a very successful theatrical star on Broadway ("Les Miserables" and now "Beauty & The Beast") and on London's West End ("Grease.") From the looks of it, there is no telling where this first explosion of success is going to take the lovely and charming Ms. Rimes, but it is certain to be both big and successful.

In spite of her young age, she is no shy shrinking violet. According to her, it is hard—if not impossible—to be in show business and be shy. She is not the manipulated product of a "stage mother" or a "stage father," like the ones of the real-life "Gypsy" Rose Lee or The Jackson Five. Nor were her parents even remotely related to show business as in the case of Liza Minnelli, or Michael Douglas, or Jane Fonda. Both of her parents—Wilbur and Belinda Rimes—attest to the fact that this was all a product of LeAnn's own determination, skill, and will.

She knew what she wanted, and she "went for it" with the gusto, drive and determination of an adult. From a very early age, she became fixated on a goal. She decided that she was going to grow up and become a singing star, and ever since that time, she and her parents have made all of the right moves to make certain that it happened exactly that way.

The song "Blue" was a critical element in the now-legendary career of LeAnn Rimes. However, the power, force and emotion that she put into her recording of that song, assured her gigantic success. It was so dynamic, in fact, that she could also have easily become a "one-hit wonder." Yet, she has managed to make one brilliant career move after another.

Musical history in the last 50 years is littered with people who became instantly successful with one hit recording, and then promptly vanished from the scene. Singer/songwriter Janis Ian had a huge hit when she was only 17, with the song "Society's Child" in the 1960's, but then was unable to follow it up until the middle of the 1970's. On the country side of things, Bobbie Gentry's block buster hit, "Ode To Billie Joe" in 1967, was such a huge success, that she NEVER could top it. The same fate could have easily befallen LeAnn Rimes. However, in less than 24 months since the single "Blue" topped the Country charts in "Billboard" magazine, young Ms. Rimes has racked up success after success with subsequent hits like "One Way Ticket (Because I Can)" and "How Do I Live."

Like so many successful singing stars, even at her young age, LeAnn Rimes' road to fame was not a product of "instant success." Although it may have looked that way from the outside, years and years of work came before she scored her first national hit with "Blue." As LeAnn herself explains, "Having a hit record is exciting. But, the suddenness of 'Blue' didn't happen overnight. Even though things have fallen into place fast since I signed my record contract, I've been singing for eight years—and I've worked hard." (B)

Along with fame, comes a certain amount of drama and trauma as well. Along the road to LeAnn's fame, there have been some hardships related to her success. It was not long after LeAnn won her 1997 Grammy Awards, that there were rumblings in the press about her parents' seemingly-sound marriage crumbling.

Apparently, the pressures of LeAnn's phenomenal success have taken their toll on the Rimes family. Now, in her second year as a star, her parents, Belinda and Wilbur, have announced that they are separating. Although it seems like this occurrence could be devastating to the 15-year-old girl, LeAnn knows in her heart that both her Mom and Dad love her dearly, and she seems to be both accepting and supportive of their decision.

Unless you have been living under a rock the last two years, and have somehow missed the unmistakable country/blues sound of LeAnn's phenomenal song "Blue," you are aware of who she is, and how powerful and gifted a singer she has proven herself to be. But few realize what a "child prodigy" she was, even at the age of five years old. How did she become a star so fast, and so successfully? How did she land her first recording contract at the age of eleven!? How has she handled the pressures of success? What are her plans and her goals? How does it feel not to have any friends her own age, and to count Reba McEntire and Wynonna Judd as her contemporaries? What is the truth about her relationship with young country hunk Bryan White? Does she miss not having a normal childhood with parties and proms? And, what does the future hold for LeAnn Rimes, when she seemingly has it all at her fingertips right this minute?

To answer all of these questions we have to go beyond her growing up years in suburban Dallas, all of the way back to rural Mississippi, where it all began...

chapter one

FROM THE BEGINNING

Musical legends have a habit of springing up in the most unlikely places. Madonna's childhood was spent in the automotive town of Pontiac, Michigan. Before she was a star, Tanya Tucker lived with her family in a trailer park in Arizona. And the legend of LeAnn Rimes began in tiny Flowood, Mississippi—population 2,860.

In was in that area, in the late 1960's, that her parents, Wilbur and Belinda grew up, and as teenagers they became high school sweethearts. Wilbur made a living selling drilling equipment for an oil company, while Belinda brought home a paycheck as a receptionist.

Together, they had a nice life, but there was something missing. They longed to have a child. A dozen wedding anniversaries came and went, and still, they seemed to be unable to produce a child. Finally, according to Belinda, she turned to religion. She began praying to God for an answer. According to her, "Within six weeks, I was pregnant with LeAnn." (O)

It was on August 28, 1982, in Jackson, Mississippi that LeAnn Rimes was born. As Belinda explains it, "We were married for 12 years before she was born, and we were told we could not have children. So when she came along, we just devoted our whole life to her." (F)

So thrilled was Belinda that she finally had the child she had longed for, that she devoted much of her time to caring for infant LeAnn, and would often sing songs to her. When the child was 18 months old, Belinda was startled to hear little LeAnn chime in and join her mother sing the spiritual ballad "Jesus Loves Me."

Soon afterwards, Wilbur had a similar experience with his baby girl. He was attempting to yodel his way through the song "All Around The Water Tank," and LeAnn began yodeling along with him. From that point on, LeAnn began singing every chance she got. She was so good at mimicking her parents in song, that they began turning on the portable cassette tape recorder to preserve some of her first "performances" merely for posterity. Little did they know at the time, but they were sitting on a gold mine!

In fact, the child liked to sing so much, that her mother was later to proclaim, "It was like LeAnn knew what she came into this world wanting to do!" (N)

Although her second album was subtitled "The Early Years," in actuality her first recordings by far predate those heard on that million-selling album—which she recorded when she was 11 years old. Her father, Wilbur, still has a cassette with LeAnn singing "Jesus Loves Me" and "You Are My Sunshine," at the astonishing age of 18 months. "I've got it on tape," he proudly proclaims. (L)

LeAnn laughs, "[Those recordings are] really funny because you can understand what I'm saying when I'm singing, but when I'm talking, you can't understand a word!" (L)

The girl was so talented as a singer, that Wilbur made it a habit of preserving several of her young performances on cassette. "She's just got a gift," he recalls. "She came here [on Earth] with it. I've [also] got tapes of her when she was two years old. I'd pick up the guitar, and she'd sing along." (G)

Although neither of them knew much about the show business world, Wilbur and Belinda did recognize their daughter's vocal gift, and began to encourage her in any way they could. They enrolled her in dance classes, and gave her every opportunity they could, to develop her talent.

The first song that LeAnn recalls performing in front of an audience is the song "Getting To Know You" from the Broadway musical, "The King & I."

"I started taking tap lessons when I was two," she explains, "and my dance teacher heard me sing one day and said, 'We need to get you into some song and dance competitions.' So, I started doing that, and 'Getting To Know You' was one of the songs I did a little dance routine to, and I sang half of it." (R)

Through all of this, Wilbur kept the the family's tape machine rolling. "My dad has tapes of me doing 'You Are My Sunshine,' 'Getting To Know You,' and 'Have Mercy' by The Judds," she points out proudly. (S)

She also recalls going to her grandmother's house as a child, where she would sit and listen to records for hours on end. It was there that she discovered all sorts of music that appealed to her. Speaking of her musical influences, LeAnn points out, "Anywhere from Barbra Streisand to Patsy Cline, you know. First I started listening to Barbra Streisand and Judy Garland, and then I started getting into Patsy Cline and Reba [McEntire] and then Wynonna [Judd]. So, those are probably the biggest influences on me." (R)

However, there was one singer in particular who had a profound effect on the way LeAnn learned to really belt, and "sell" a song. According to her, "Patsy Cline was one of the first country music artists I listened to. I love her music, especially 'Crazy.' She's been a big influence!" (B) Little did she know at the time, but there was going to be a significant tie to the legendary Cline, one that would help launch her career.

At the age of five, LeAnn sang a full version of her tap dancing song, "Getting To Know You," that virtually astounded her parents. Time and time again they were awed by her singing ability. Wilbur and Belinda couldn't help but become aware of the fact that their daughter truly had something very special.

Was LeAnn always destined for stardom? Well, by 1988 it sure began to look that way—on an ever increasing basis. When she was all of six years old, she announced to her parents that she was going to grow up and become a singer, and be "bigger than Barbra Streisand!" (A)

By the time she was six, LeAnn was already making the rounds of all the local talent shows in the area. One night her mother drove her daughter to one of the most important ones, while Wilbur went off on his own, to go raccoon hunting. He got home ahead of the girls. When he caught the sight of little LeAnn struggling to carry the six-foot-tall First Prize trophy through the door, it literally brought tears to his eyes.

After the excitement subsided, Wilbur said to his only child, "Come over here and talk to me, LeAnn. Is this what you want to do?" (F)

LeAnn looked back at him and honestly replied, "Oh, yes, Daddy, it's all I ever want." (F)

Well, that was "it." Wilbur and Belinda made plans to move out of Mississippi, to a town where there were bigger and better stakes for little LeAnn.

Belinda explains of her daughter, "She was always strong-willed, and she was this-away—straight ahead, focused. When you've got a kid like that and you're not like that yourself, it kind of makes you that way. When you've been laid-back and easygoing, you've gotta go with the flow and see what happens." (F) It was a gamble, but all three of them unanimously agreed on the move, and they never looked back to Mississippi once: they loaded up the car, and they moved to "Big D"— Dallas that is—oil wells and country music shows galore.

While she was still only six, she auditioned for the title role in the Broadway-bound musical "Annie 2." She nearly landed the part on the power of her singing alone. This audition also helped to give her "the acting bug." This bent in her young and blossoming career has come to full fruition with her 1997 film "Holiday In Your Heart." Actually, it is just as well that she didn't land the role in the "Annie" sequel. "Annie 2" ended up eaten alive by the critics, and did not end up anywhere near the smashing success of the original Broadway show "Annie," nor the movie that was made from it.

One of the first places LeAnn showcased her singing talents, was on the local "Dallas Opry" circuit in Texas. Belinda recalls how exhausting these trips were for LeAnn: "She'd be sleeping in the car as we drove to the next Opry, and then she'd get up on the stage and sing 'Crazy,' and then get right back in the car and go to sleep." (I) The Opry would tour around, playing local dates in greater metropolitan Dallas, fondly known as the "Metroplex" area. Rimes was seen singing

16

in nearby Garland, Mesquite, Greenville, and Grapevine. She also performed at local rodeo events, and anywhere else she could find a platform for her talent.

Although she was only six years old, LeAnn and her parents began assembling her own touring band to perform with. Several of the key members of her band are still with her to this very day. They have become more like family members to her than they are band members.

Whenever she wasn't singing—which was rarely—LeAnn's other extracurricular activities also included T-ball, and gymnastics. She seemed to have boundless energy, even for a girl her age.

Many people recall having experiences as a child, that touch them in a profound way. Explaining one she remembers, LeAnn claims, "I've always wanted to help children in some way. I had a neighbor, an Asian man, who was deaf. One of my friends went up to talk to him, and she taught me sign language. So I got to talk to him in that way and became friends with him. I thought that

was something neat, to work with deaf people and people who have speech problems." (T) To this day, she claims that if and when she attends college, she might pursue Speech Therapy as one of her major courses of study.

Her parents were thrilled with the vocal charisma, determination, and stamina that their daughter displayed on stage. In a very short period of time, it escalated from a creative hobby, and began to show promise as an actual life long career move for the young girl. Her mother explains, "When LeAnn was 7 years old, I realized her singing was a special gift that God gave her. I knew she was going to be successful in the recording business, because somebody would recognize her voice for what it is." (B) Both Wilbur and Belinda continued to seek out new avenues for their daughter to showcase her talent.

It was at the age of seven that LeAnn began performing regularly in a local talent revue, which was then based in Fort Worth, Texas, called The Johnnie High Country Revue, which has been running over 23 years now. (It has since relocated to nearby Arlington, Texas). "She had poise, dedication, and stage presence," Johnnie High recalls of being absolutely amazed by LeAnn's power and self-confidence on stage. "She didn't look like a pageant girl. She looked like a country singer, and she just come out [on stage] and done it!" (I)

In December of 1989, at the age of seven, LeAnn made her theatrical acting debut in a local Dallas production of the musical version of Charles Dickens' "A Christmas Carol." She was one of the stars of the production, portraying the character of Tiny Tim.

When LeAnn was eight years old, she appeared on the national TV talent show, "Star Search," and ended up winning the top prize two weeks in a row. The song she sang to win with, was the old Marty Robbins hit, "Don't Worry About Me."

That same year, Wilbur arranged for LeAnn to have her first recording session, just so she would get the feel of singing in a glass booth, without an audience to play off of, and perform for. At the age of ten, she had her second practice session in the recording studio.

Ask any singer, and they will almost unanimously tell you that the most difficult song of all to sing, is the American National Anthem, "The Star Spangled Banner." However, even as a child, LeAnn could breeze through it "a capella"—which means without any musical accompaniment at all. During this era LeAnn found herself on stage launching into "The Star Spangled Banner" before stadium crowds at the Walt Garrison Rodeo, the National Cutting Horse Championship in Fort Worth, and at Dallas Cowboy games, with both style and confidence.

Following her career, step by step, both of her parents could plainly see that their daughter was growing and developing as a professional performer. Although she was extremely young, once LeAnn was up on stage, she was able to sing a song with all of the gusto and finesse of a singer more than twice her age. Finally, it was time for eleven-year-old LeAnn Rimes to make her leap into becoming a full-fledged recording artist.

chapter two

THE EARLY YEARS

*T*he great thing about performing at a well-attended event like the Dallas Cowboys football games, is the fact that you never know what important people are in attendance, watching you. It was at one of these events that a local disk jockey named Bill Mack witnessed one of LeAnn's showstopping performances of the National Anthem. As Mack himself recalls, "At 11 years old, it was frightening how unbelievably good she was!" (N)

In addition to being a local disk jockey, on station WBAP in Dallas, Bill Mack had also dabbled in songwriting early in his career. In the 1960's he wrote a song called "Drinking Champagne," which he penned with singer Dean Martin in mind. It ended up being recorded by country singer Cal Smith in the late '60's, instead of by Martin. In the late 1950's, while working for a Wichita Falls, Kansas radio station; Mack had written a song called "Blue," which he intended to have super singer Patsy Cline record.

In 1960, Mack had since changed jobs, and found himself in San Antonio, Texas, working for another radio station, when it was announced that a country show was coming to town, headlined by none other than Roger Miller and Patsy Cline. Through his radio station affiliation, Mack found himself backstage with both Miller and Cline. He told Patsy that he had a song that he wrote with her in mind, called "Blue." When Cline asked him how it went, Mack borrowed Roger Miller's guitar, and launched into several bars of it for Patsy.

According to Mack, the vivacious Patsy Cline not only listened to his tune, but liked it right then and there on the spot. When he was finished, he claims that she looked him squarely in the eyes and commanded, "Get that damn thing to me!" (I) Mack told her that he would have a "demo" recording made of the song, and send it on to her. By the time he got the song cut by a local singer, and forwarded it to Nashville, it somehow got lost in the shuffle.

In March of 1963, Patsy Cline was killed in a horrible plane crash. All of Mack's hopes of the song "Blue" ever reaching its full potential, died along with her that tragic day.

In the late 1980's, another Fort Worth singer, by the name of Polly Stephens, recorded a torch version of "Blue." She pressed it, and she would sell copies of it after her local Texas gigs. Still, Mack was not satisfied that the song had been performed as he had intended it to sound.

When Bill Mack heard LeAnn Rimes singing the National Anthem before the Dallas Cowboys' game at Texas Stadium in Irving, he had to strain to see if this huge voice was really coming out of an 11-year-old child. According to him, "I thought she was a 30-year-old midget! I said, 'She's gotta hear 'Blue.'" (T)

Mack made a beeline right over to the stage to find out who this young singer was, because he immediately thought of how close to Patsy Cline's voice, LeAnn's sounded. He claims that before Rimes came along, "[Patsy Cline] was the only one I could hear sing it." (O) Mack met LeAnn and her parents and told them about the song "Blue," which he had written, and they agreed to give it a listen.

Within a week the Rimes family received the demo for the song, and together they gave it a listen. "I knew 'Blue' was perfect for me," LeAnn recalls of her reaction to it, the second she heard it. She knew that it was a hit, and she instantly loved it. (P)

However, Wilbur's reaction was completely different. According to LeAnn, "My dad heard the tape and threw it in the corner. He said it was 'too old' for me. But I kept bugging him about it. I stuck it back in the tape recorder and said, 'I love that.' Then, I got the idea to put that yodel thing to it." (G) It was an inspired move that even Patsy Cline would approve of, because "the Cline" herself would often put such countrified touches in her own early recordings.

LeAnn further explains, "My dad said the song was too old for me. I loved it, though, and I kept bugging him about it." (S)

In retrospect, Wilbur Rimes admits, "'Blue' I didn't like it. But it was a demo version that sounded old-fashioned. LeAnn added the yodel and then I fell in love with it. She really transformed the song." (P)

It was during this same era, in 1993 that it was decided that LeAnn's career demands were disrupting her schoolwork. So, instead of pulling the plug on her singing, LeAnn started enlisting a tutor, and she quit attending school. That way she could continue to meet the demands of her blossoming career, without sacrificing her education.

There was however, another reason for LeAnn dropping out of school. Junior high school kids can be very mean, and because Rimes was a local star in the Dallas area, she found herself ridiculed and "threatened a lot." As she explains it, "I had a lot of friends, but there were these four girls who were scaring me sometimes." (Y)

Such a move might be looked upon as Belinda and Wilbur forcing their will for their daughter's career upon her. Quite the contrary, LeAnn explains, "I pushed my parents more than they pushed me. They've never been backstage parents. I told them what I wanted to do." (B)

Now, free from the constraints of her school's schedule, and anxious to get LeAnn into the mainstream recording business, the family traveled to Nashville, where they met with the head of EMI Music, Jimmy Bowen. "I sang at his house," she recalls, "but he told me to come back when I was 18 because he didn't want to take on a child, because he thought I wasn't really old enough right now to handle it." (H) Although she was disappointed at the time, she explains, "I know I was kinda ready then, but I wasn't really. He was right to tell me to wait, but I wanted it." (I)

chapter two

With all of this activity happening around her it wasn't long before another opportunity for a legitimate recording session came her way. Through LeAnn's constant performances in the area, the Rimes family had become acquainted with a Dallas attorney by the name of Lyle Walker. In addition to his law practice, Walker was also the part owner—along with Norman Petty—of a famous recording studio, located in Clovis, New Mexico. The studio was the site where rock legend Buddy Holly recorded most of his biggest hits. That original studio is now a famed tourist attraction. In addition to owning that museum of a studio, Walker and Petty also owned another studio, which was located in a reconverted movie theater in Clovis.

Walker put up his own money to bankroll the recording of a full album of music by little 11-year-old LeAnn Rimes. While the family was there, the young girl put her unmistakable voice to the album's worth of tracks they recorded. Due to his putting up the money for the recording of the album, Lyle Walker became co-manager in the girl's career, along with Wilbur Rimes.

The main number on LeAnn's agenda was recording the song "Blue." She had finally worked on her father long enough, that he finally relented, and acquiesced into letting her record it—her way. This first version of "Blue," became the showpiece of the album, which was ultimately entitled "All That."

THE EARLY YEARS

Also included on "All That," was Patsy Montana's trademark hit from the 1930's, "I Want To Be A Cowboy's Sweetheart." Rimes also put her personal stamp on Dolly Parton's classic "I Will Always Love You," Bill Monroe's "Blue Moon Of Kentucky," The Beatles' "Yesterday," and the song "Unchained Melody," which had been a hit for—among other artists—The Righteous Brothers.

Another of the album's highlights was LeAnn's first self-penned composition, "Share My Love," which she wrote with Blake Vickers. Other cuts on the album included "River Of Love," "The Rest Is History," "Broken Wing," and "Sure Thing."

When "All That" was completed, it was released on an independent label called NorVaJak. Through Lyle Walker's connections, the Blockbuster video and music chain in the Dallas/Metroplex area carried the LP. By now, LeAnn was becoming something of a local legend. So much so, that her "All That" album sold an incredible 15,000 copies. (Original copies of it have since gone on to become something of a Rimes collector's item!)

Now that LeAnn was becoming known as a Dallas household name, it was time to catapult her onto the national market. In other words: Today Dallas, Tomorrow the World!

chapter three
THE "BLUE" ALBUM

*T*he year 1995 was a really big one for LeAnn Rimes, her first album, "All That" was a hit in Dallas, she turned twelve years old, and she made over 100 concert appearances in the area. One of her biggest thrills of the year came when she was the opening act for Randy Travis, at the Starplex in Dallas. Things were heating up month by month. LeAnn could feel the excitement and the energy mounting around her.

Representatives from the Nashville offices of several major record companies were suddenly expressing interest in signing LeAnn to a long-term recording contract. During this same period of time, Rimes performed a showcase at a local theater for executives from Decca Records.

Meanwhile, Mike Curb, president of Curb Records in Nashville, Tennessee, recalls, "Someone sent me her CD, I put it on and everyone just turned their heads!" (S) Instinctively, he could tell that there was hit-making potential right there. Curb wasn't one who was at a loss as to what to do with young talent. Among his biggest selling stars of the 1970's and 1980's were Marie Osmond, and Debby Boone. Instead of LeAnn's young age being a deterrent, it was considered an asset in Mike Curb's eyes. Encouraged by his own teenage daughters to sign LeAnn, Curb got into contact with Wilbur Rimes. Wilbur emphasized to Curb how important it was to him that he personally look out for his daughter by continuing as her manager, and her record producer, because no one knew LeAnn or her voice like he did. Curb wasn't put off by this request. In fact, he rather liked the whole family connection.

LeAnn and her parents liked the offer that Mike Curb made to them, and accepted it. With that, the wheels were set in motion for the big push to launch her career on a national and international basis.

Mike Curb especially loved the sound of the song "Blue," and wanted to make it the centerpiece of the album. However, before he released it, it was decided that LeAnn should go back into the recording studio, and cut a new version. As Wilbur explains it, they wanted to have a fresh rendition of the song, with "her thirteen-year-old voice instead of her eleven-year-old voice." (I)

The other ten selections that they chose to accompany "Blue" on the album were also drawn from a roster of songs that are decidedly "adult," and not the type of songs that one would expect coming out of the mouth of a 13-year-old girl. For instance, on the song "My Baby," LeAnn is heard singing about her boyfriend as her "lover," one who is a fully grown man. On "Hurt," LeAnn believably laments the loss of a love affair, and on "One Way Ticket (Because I Can)" she sings about breaking up with her boyfriend, and hopping on the next plane. These aren't exactly the kind of songs that one would expect to be sung by a young girl who is only 13. First of all, how on Earth would a child that age know of the misery of heartbreak, or the loss of a lover?

THE "BLUE" ALBUM

With regard to the song selections on the "Blue" album, LeAnn firmly explained, "I don't want people to think of me as a thirteen-year-old singing sensation. I want them to think of me only as an artist and for my music, so that I will have the freedom to do the songs I like. If I sing little kid songs about getting out of high school and stuff like that, I'm never gonna make it. I'm trying to appeal to everybody from four to eighty." (I)

The one song that could have been believably sung by a young teenager, was LeAnn's duet version of the old Eddy Arnold hit, "Cattle Call," which was done as a duet with Arnold himself. It's inclusion helped to give the album a touch of balance, in that every song wasn't a mournful lament of lost love.

It was, however, kind of an odd stretch to team a 13-year-old with a 78-year-old, but somehow it worked. Referring to their friendship, LeAnn said of Arnold, "At first I was his 'granddaughter,' then I graduated to his 'daughter.' He is a very, very, nice guy." (Y)

Speaking about her formula for adding adult emotions to a song, she reveals, "Dad would explain that it was a sad song, and I could sing it that way. I don't think I have to experience anything to sing it." (O)

Listening to the finished product, it is amazing to think that half of the time she didn't even understand some of the emotions that the songwriter put into them. "I don't think I have to live a song, really, to sing it," she proclaims. "I think I'm kind of like how an actor interprets a script: I interpret a song. If I fall in love with the music and the overall song, I just think, 'I want to sing that,' but I know what they're talking about, I do. I mean, I've seen people get hurt before. My close friends have gotten hurt, and I know what they're going through." (F) Whatever the formula, it sure works for her, so, she shouldn't change a thing!

In rerecording the song "Blue," 13-year-old Ms. Rimes really nailed down the definitive version of the song, making it even more sincere and heartbreaking than the rendition that was on the original "All That" album. Says LeAnn, "I think it was an honor to have a song that was written for Patsy—I mean, she's been a big influence on me. And it's a big honor to live up to the writer's expectations of the song, you know, what he thought the song should sound like—you know, to live up to that." (R) Even Patsy Cline herself would have been happy with the wonderful job LeAnn did.

From the moment that one hears the song "Blue," one cannot help but compare LeAnn's performance to that of the legendary Patsy Cline. Since Cline met her untimely death in 1963, Rimes ponders, "I've been compared with her so many times, and I know a lot about her, but I wish I could have met her to learn more. She's passed away, so that's one thing I can't do." (K)

No one was more pleased with the way it came out than the songwriter himself. According to Bill Mack, "People call what she does with her voice a yodel, but it's not like some Swiss yodeler—it's really what we call a 'soul break.' It's something tuggin' at you." (F)

Originally, her record company was going to save "Blue" for later release as a single. However, Curb Records sent out 10-second samples of the song for feedback from country radio stations across America. The listener response was so phenomenal that the company was forced to scrap the idea of releasing the song "The Light In Your Eyes" first, and they immediately started pressing copies of "Blue," by popular demand.

In April of 1996, radio station WMZQ, the largest country radio station in the Washington D.C. area, received a special "preview" copy of the single "Blue." According to WMZQ's Program Director, Mac Daniels, "I gave it to our nighttime guy, Scott Carpenter, and said, 'Take this, have some fun with it. He played it that night and the response was so overwhelming, he had to play it three times. It was kids calling, kids' grandparents calling. The next day, the morning D.J., Gary Murphy, comes to me, and says, 'What's this "Blue" song? We're getting a ton of calls. We need to play it!' And, he played it, and it kept snowballing." (F)

THE "BLUE" ALBUM

chapter three

In May of 1996, right after the single version of "Blue" was released and began leapfrogging its way up the radio airplay charts, LeAnn confessed to Rick Mitchell of the "Houston Chronicle," "I really don't know what's going to happen. I'm just taking it day by day. I really didn't expect my first single to take off like this. It's amazing to me, to see what's its done." (G)

"Blue" became an instant smash of a record, going on to become the fastest added single in country music since Billy Ray Cyrus broke his "Achy Breaky Heart." Recalls LeAnn, "I heard myself played on the radio in Dallas a few times before the song was released, but when I really heard it outside of Dallas, it was in Nashville and I heard it on a station up in Nashville and I was really excited about it. It was really neat!" (R)

Watching the care that Curb Records took in positioning and launching LeAnn's first single release, the teenager was thrilled to break free of the constraints of being known only as a regional star in Dallas. "I think there's a lot of great artists who have come out of Texas, but I'm going for broader appeal. I was very skeptical when 'Blue' was released as a single because it was very traditional, and I knew radio was gonna be hesitant to play it. They call it 'retro,' but it's true country music and it's totally different from contemporary country, which has the pop feel," she says. (I)

"Blue" debuted in "Billboard" magazine at Number 49—with a bullet—in their May 25, 1996 issue. The next week, it charted at Number 36. It didn't stop climbing until it reached the top of the chart. Not only was it an instant hit in the Country arena, but it also crossed over to the pop stations, peaking at Number Three on the Pop chart.

Suddenly, LeAnn Rimes was all over the airwaves, and quickly becoming a nationally known household name. She admitted at the time, "I think we knew it was a good song, but I didn't know it would be this big of a hit." (M)

On June 11, LeAnn performed for 24,000 fans at Nashville's famed annual event, Fan Fair. "The Washington Post" quoted her rushing off stage and exclaiming, "They know my song, Mom!" (F) TV's "Good Morning America" started calling to book her, "People" magazine was phoning, wanting to do a profile. On June 23 she performed at the Bull Run Jamboree with Collin Ray and Aaron Tippin, then returned to the "Metroplex" area to headline at Billy Bob's in Fort Worth, Texas. She was already secured to perform several upcoming dates as an opening act for Wynonna Judd, and for the country group Blackhawk. Suddenly, she was in the bigtime!

People from Philadelphia to Phoenix were startled to find out that the song "Blue," was indeed by a girl in the first full year of her teens. That summer LeAnn told "The New York Times," "I think the reason I don't act or sound 13, is that I've grown up in an adult world my whole life. Those are who my friends are." (D)

According to Belinda Rimes at the time, "I'm just amazed. Absolutely amazed—and a nervous wreck." (U) Ironically, it was LeAnn who was the calm and confident one in the family.

The album "Blue" debuted on "Billboard" magazine's Top Country Albums at Number One the week of July 27, 1996, and it began racking up sales figures at an astonishing rate. LeAnn Rimes was still only 13 years old at the time, and already she was an instant success!

1996: AN INCREDIBLE YEAR

*O*n August 28, 1996, LeAnn Rimes celebrated her 14th birthday a virtual singing mogul. She was garnering so much publicity and airplay, she was being looked upon as a "cottage industry" unto herself.

This was so true, that on that very day she found herself on the cover of the "Marketplace" section of daily financial Bible "The Wall Street Journal." According to the article, entitled "Singin' an Oldie, She's Lookin' Like A Star," it was the Patsy Cline connection to the song "Blue," which really galvanized radio support around her. It referred to "the Cline" (as Patsy would refer to herself), as being "revered almost religiously." (X)

As for LeAnn's across-the-board success and Cline comparisons, "The Wall Street Journal" claimed, "Miss Rimes, who turns 14 years old today, doesn't look or always sound like the country queen known for smoky heartbreakers like 'Crazy' and 'I Fall To Pieces.' But the young singer does have 'Blue,' a ballad originally written for Ms. Cline...Miss Rimes's album by the same name made its debut as Number One on 'Billboard' magazine's country-music chart when it was released last month, and it remains Number One today. Her live concerts now draw huge crowds." (X)

Most girls on their 14th birthday would be happy with a new outfit for their Barbie doll, a new diary to write in, or a new record by their favorite singing star. Instead, LeAnn Rimes found herself more famous than Barbie, living a show business life that spun so fast she didn't have time to write into a diary, and instead of collecting or playing hit albums—she was recording them!

Indeed, breathing the rarefied air of the country music Mount Olympus upon which she had just ascended, made young LeAnn Rimes a true legend in her own time, and unique even amongst her peers. That summer she was able to honestly proclaim, "There's not a day that's gone by for the past month that I haven't been doing something. I've been doing this since I was five, so its never been a really typical life. But this is the way I've grown up in an adult world all my life, and a lot of my friends are between 20 and 80, basically, some of them are in the business, and some aren't. But most of them are." (H)

Not long after "Blue" became a huge smash on the Country and Pop charts, her next single, "Hurt Me," was already hitting the charts. LeAnn was well on her way to becoming something of a singing legend, long before she was even eligible to obtain her driver's license!

Ever since she graduated from Sixth Grade, stopped attending junior high school and began working with a personal tutor, she knew nothing about being a typical teenager. All of her experiences were truly those of an adult. "I really haven't had any friends my age since I stopped going to public school three years ago," she says. (M)

★

chapter four

★

1996: AN INCREDIBLE YEAR

Not since Brenda Lee in the 1950's and Tanya Tucker in the 1970's had the country music world seen such a young and promising superstar. LeAnn was making such headlines with her Number One album and Number One debut single, that the comparisons to Lee and Tucker abounded in the press. Rimes' story was such big news that neither of Brenda nor Tanya could miss the attention that was being showered upon her.

Speaking of LeAnn, Brenda claims, "Her voice is phenomenal on 'Blue'—she certainly doesn't sound like she's 13. When they said on the radio that she was 13, my jaw dropped." (B)

Having also lived through the pressure of becoming a teenage star at a young age, what advice did Lee have for Rimes? "The first thing I would tell her is to finish her education, especially high school," Brenda emphasized. "Don't let anything stand in the way of that. College is a plus if you can do it, but it's important to be with kids your own age and experience the things you would experience if you weren't singing and having some success and all that that brings." (B)

Expressing concern for LeAnn, Brenda also offered the piece of advice: "If people around her treat her as a person and not a product, I think she'll be fine." (B)

Similarly, Tanya Tucker proclaims, "I think LeAnn is a good singer and I'm happy for her success. It's been a long time since we've heard a Patsy Cline influence, so I think it's great that LeAnn has that feel to her voice." (B)

Known as something of a hellion as a child and as a young adult, Tanya offered further insights by stating, "I'm amazed it's taken this long for someone else to make this kind of debut. But, I think it's well deserved. My advice to LeAnn is to stick with at least two subjects in school: English, which will give her confidence in talking with the press, and history. She needs to know where she came from before she knows where she's going." (D)

On the subject of being compared with these two country legends, LeAnn commented, "It's great to be mentioned with Brenda and Tanya, but the fact that we started our recording careers when we were young is the only real comparison." (B) She felt uniquely like her own person, and she preferred to be thought of as "LeAnn," and in contrast to others who came before her.

1996: AN INCREDIBLE YEAR

After the excitement of hitting Number One, and turning fourteen had subsided, it was back to business. One of the most exciting aspects of her life in the second half of 1996, came with working alongside some of her favorite stars, including Vince Gill, Wynonna Judd, and young country hunk Bryan White. She became one of the hottest opening acts of the year, joining several major tours already in progress. On August 8, 1996 she began headlining for Dwight Yoakam, in San Diego. On August 13 she joined Vince Gill in Nashville, then Wynonna on August 30 in Cleveland, and Alan Jackson on October 30 in Albuquerque.

Being Wynonna's opening act was especially exciting for LeAnn, and she was very verbal about what a great honor that was. Wynonna returned the compliment by proclaiming of Rimes, "That girl is awesome!" (Y)

LeAnn recalls, "I toured with Wynonna and became very good friends with her. I know Reba very well too. To have them come up and say they really like your album and your music is...I mean, I've listened to them forever, and to have them say that to me is a big thrill." (T)

When asked what kind of advice Reba McEntire and Wynonna Judd had for her, LeAnn explained, "Really, just to keep my head on straight and take time for myself and have fun." (T)

In October 31, 1996, LeAnn found herself in Tucson, Arizona, on the concert bill with Alan Jackson, and Emilio. However, of all the people she had recently met, young hunk Bryan White eclipsed them all. In her gossip and news column in the "Tucson Citizen," writer A.J. Flick revealed, "It's Nashville's worst-kept secret that LeAnn has a crush on Bryan. Well, what girl her age wouldn't? LeAnn's not the only one getting ribbed about this puppy love. Vince [Gill] says he's kidding Bryan relentlessly." (W)

Laughingly, Vince—who was in Tucson at the time—told Flick, "I've been teasin' her since she's been here [in Tucson]. I got her homework done. And I got her a Bryan White lunch box to take home." (W)

1996: AN INCREDIBLE YEAR

With regards to the Halloween show in "the Old Pueblo," country music critic A.J. Flick proclaimed, "This young lady has the pipes, songwriting talent and versatility to be a major musical force." (Z)

That autumn, LeAnn also flew to "the land down under," to make her first appearances on the continent of Australia. She took great delight in watching her name climb up the international music charts. "This is like my personal record," LeAnn gushed delightfully. "The biggest highlight is seeing that people like my music in the U.S., Australia...everywhere! Every day it's get up, do interviews, sound check, do a show, and go to the next place. We've been home in Dallas six days since the first of June. To put it in one word, it's been 'crazy!'" (E)

When the Country Music Association Awards were presented on October 2, 1996, LeAnn Rimes was chosen to perform at the opening of the nationally telecast show. According to Vince Gill, of all of the artists the CMA's might have chosen for such an honor, "[LeAnn Rimes was] the most deserved artist of all." (W) Not only was she the show's opening act, but she was also nominated for two of the top awards: The Horizon Award, and Single Of The Year for "Blue."

According to her at the time, "I'm skeptical about how my career's gonna go, but I'm very excited. Being nominated for two CMA awards, that's like the biggest highlight of my life, 'cause that's what I've dreamed about since I was a little girl sitting in front of the TV watching Reba get an award." (I)

Imagine her surprise when she won both awards when they were handed out on Wednesday, October 3, 1996. The Horizon Award is given annually to the country music performer whose career has made the furthest advancement in the past year. Considering that she had taken the entire country music world by storm in a matter of only four months—who was more deserving than she? Since its debut on the "Billboard" Country Album charts in July, LeAnn's album had become the biggest selling LP to grace those charts. Not only did it hit Number One in July, but it also remained there an astonishing 20 weeks during the rest of 1996. Never before in country music history, had an album by a 13-year-old singer accomplished such a feat!

As 1996 came to a close, LeAnn was able to proclaim, "This year was a little overwhelming. I didn't know what to expect with my first single and my album. 'Blue' was so different from what everybody was playing that people were loving it. It's been a dream come true: I've been wanting to do this ever since I was five!" (E)

All of the excitement that LeAnn's career stirred up might have been upsetting to some families, but for the Rimes clan, it seemed to draw them closer to each other. "This has been really fun for my whole family," LeAnn said at the time. (M) For her, the fun had just begun!

chapter five

THE "INSPIRATIONAL" ALBUM

*A*s 1997 began, LeAnn Rimes' "Blue" album was still Number One on "Billboard" magazine's Country Albums chart—for its 22nd week. She really had to feel accomplished, keeping the likes of Reba McEntire, Alan Jackson, Clint Black, Brooks & Dunn, and Garth Brooks from hitting the top of the charts! At the age of 14 she was the reigning Queen of Country, and the stakes were only beginning to heat up for her already "RED HOT" career.

With the "Blue" album sitting contently at Number One, the other LP's in the Top Ten included: 2. "Did I Shave My Legs For This?" by Deana Carter, 3. "Greatest Hits" by Brooks & Dunn, 4. "Everything I Love" by Alan Jackson, 5. "What If It's You" by Reba McEntire, 6. "The Woman In Me" by Shania Twain, 7. "Borderline" by Brooks & Dunn, 8. "The Hits" by Garth Brooks, 9. "Measure Of A Man" by Kevin Sharp, and 10. "Ten Thousand Angels" by Mindy McCready. Even more significantly, LeAnn Rimes was going to have not one—but two—additional million-selling albums hitting the Number One slot before the year was up!

As the epitome of the old saying, "strike while the iron is hot," while LeAnn was still sailing fast and high on the rush of success from her debut LP, Curb Records released her second nationally distributed album. In a way, her second Curb album was also her "first." The album was ultimately entitled "Unchained Melody / The Early Years."

Listening to the album, this was clearly a "preview of coming attractions" for LeAnn's now-established career. It contains all sorts of evidence of stretching out her wings by trying several different vocal techniques, and musical approaches for the preteen songstress. There is yodeling country, torchy power ballads, and pure pop. In the two years between the recording of this album, and 1996's "Blue," LeAnn's voice had clearly grown and changed.

The album opens with Patsy Montana's signature song, "I Want To Be A Cowboy's Sweetheart," a rousing novelty song dating back to 1935, when it became the first million-selling country single ever. On the fun song of cowgirl bravado—with yelps, yips and yodeling—LeAnn obviously has a ball giving it her best "Patsy Cline / Dale Evans " "ridin' the range" gusto. It is a cute recording, and LeAnn sounds like she is believably eleven years old at the time she recorded it.

On the next number, the power ballad "I Will Always Love You," young Rimes belts out this song of love and devotion like a pro. This has twice been a Number One hit for Dolly Parton, who also penned the song. However, it was LeAnn's idol Whitney Houston, who in the early 1990's turned it into one of the biggest selling singles of all time. This country version is a wonderful rendition of one of the most popular and beautiful songs ever written.

THE "INSPIRATIONAL" ALBUM

"Blue Moon Of Kentucky," which was written by Bill Monroe, has been covered by country artists for years. This was one of Patsy Cline's favorite songs, which she recorded during her all-too-short singing career. LeAnn begins her rendition of this country/Western classic a capella, swinging into the song with lively effervescence, infusing it with a sense of lively youthful fun.

On the lamenting "River Of Love," the young country sound of "The Rest Of History," and the lovelorn "Broken Wing," LeAnn tackles more adult themes. She ably holds her own on material which tells of experiences that would be foreign to someone her young age of eleven! But, even then, she seemed to feel the emotions in the lyrics, and the mood of each song.

Singing Joyce Harrison's "Sure Thing," LeAnn sounds every inch like a seasoned pro. And, selling her own composition, "Share My Love" (written with Blake Vickers), she shows off not only her expressive voice, but her talent as a songwriter as well.

John Lennon and Paul McCartney's "Yesterday" evokes memories of a simpler age, and gives Rimes a chance at interpreting one of The Beatles' biggest hits of the 1960's. This song is one of the true highlights of the entire album. The uncluttered arrangement of this pop hit, gives LeAnn a chance to really stretch out vocally, and test her higher register.

The album is rounded out with "Unchained Melody," which finds the talented Ms. Rimes in fine form. She interprets the lush ballad with emotional fire and focused intensity, making a trademark song all her own.

Most of the press reviews were very favorable when "Unchained Melody / The Early Years" was released in February of 1997. "Time" magazine glowed, "Despite her age, the raw talent and gleaming promise of this album are apparent. Her take on the country standard 'Blue Moon of Kentucky' comes across as fresh and bracing as cold well water, and her version of 'I Will Always Love You' is equally crisp and bright. On every track, Rimes' voice resonates with a mellow center, vibrant edges and a steady glow of pure innocence." (L)

Even more outrageously, when the album was released, it debuted at Number One on not only the Country Album Chart in "Billboard" magazine, but on the Pop Album chart as well, giving her two albums in the Top Ten at once. Considering that the album "Unchained Melody / The Early Years" was recorded by an eleven-year-old, that makes LeAnn Rimes the youngest solo performer to ever top the "Billboard" album chart!

On February 27, 1997, for the first time in several years, the annual Grammy Awards telecast, emanated from New York City. Although it does bounce back and forth between the East Coast and the West Coast, most often it is held in Los Angeles. Another new aspect of this telecast was the fact that the Awards were held at Madison Square Garden for the very first time. In years past, it was usually Radio City Music Hall where they were held when they were awarded on the East Coast.

In the category of Best New Artist, LeAnn was competing with other recording world newcomers, The Tony Rich Project, Garbage, Jewel, and No Doubt. One of the most exciting things about being on the Grammy Awards show in 1997, was the fact that she had the chance to meet and rub elbows with several of her idols in the music business, both from the country music realm, as well as the pop, rock and jazz arenas. One of her favorite singing stars, Bonnie Raitt, was one whom she had the opportunity to meet and befriend. "We actually shared a dressing room at the Grammys," LeAnn explains enthusiastically. "She came up to me and said, 'I love your music.' It was pretty cool, but I don't really get starstruck anymore. Some stars are my friends, so I've figured out they're just like everybody else." (K)

It was in March, right after The Grammy Awards were handed out, that it was announced that LeAnn Rimes would be expanding her job description from "singer / songwriter" to add "author" to the growing list of her marketable talents. According to "Publishers Weekly" magazine, Rimes was paid a million dollar advance to pen her own Christmas fable, entitled "Holiday In My Heart." There was no telling what was next! On April 23, 1997, LeAnn continued her sweep of the music awards, by taking home a pair of trophies for "New Female Singer," and "Top Song" for "Blue." "I could really get used to this. This isn't too bad!" she gushed backstage after her trio of wins. "It's amazing. It's overwhelming and exciting at the same time." (BB)

The Country Music Association Awards, The Grammy Awards, and now the Academy Of Country Music Awards. This was indeed getting to be a habit with LeAnn Rimes. According to her at the time, "I really didn't expect...any of these awards. This is my first year, you know? But one of the things I really remember is the big clap when they called out my name. I used to watch 'em on TV and think, 'Maybe one day I'll be up there.' It was a blast." (T) Well, lo and behold, now it was LeAnn's turn to accept the awards!

It was in April of 1997 that rumblings started circulating in the press about a slight rift in the Rimes family. Tabloid newspaper, "The Globe," reported in its April 15 issue that LeAnn was being entangled in a bit of a tug-of-war between her parents, Belinda and Wilbur. According to its news reports, LeAnn's father/manager was urging his daughter to do all she can to get the most out of her career momentum, especially in light of all of the awards she was winning. Her mother on the other hand was reported as wanting LeAnn to relax a bit, and enjoy being a child—a time in one's life that only comes once. Part young woman, and part little girl, LeAnn didn't seem to want to take sides, but she calmly continued to pursue all of the opportunities that her blossoming career had to offer her.

Likewise, the following week, "The Star" also got into the fray. According to the story, entitled "Heartache For Teen Sensation LeAnn Rimes / She Misses TV Show As Parents Fight Over Her Career," an incident in the studios of the Nashville Network was specifically cited. According to the report, one unnamed source claimed, "There was shouting, and harsh words were flying up and down the hallway during production meetings and rehearsals. Belinda let Wilbur know she thinks he drives LeAnn too hard. Finally Belinda said, 'That's it, I'm leaving!' and stormed out of the studio." (DD) Apparently, LeAnn was so upset, that she retreated to her dressing room in tears, and canceled the TV taping. For several months to come, that was the only report of a brewing Rimes family feud.

That same month, LeAnn was one of the headliners at the Country Thunder USA festival in Queen Creek, Arizona, a three-day, four-night fete including rodeo events, shopping, and top flight country music entertainment. Also on the bill, at the event which drew over 115,000 people, were Joe Diffie, Gary Allan, Chris LeDoux, Kevin Sharp, and the group Ricochet.

On June 9, 1997 LeAnn Rimes made a surprise appearance in Tucson, Arizona, at the downtown Tucson Convention Center. Vince Gill was headlining, and his opening act was 23-year old heartthrob Bryan White. Amidst White's concert set that night, a special guest star showed up on stage for one number. It was LeAnn Rimes, dressed in a bare midriff top, decorated with fringe. She joined Bryan for a sizzling duet version of the Bonnie Raitt hit, "I Can't Make You Love Me." The duet was so steamy and vocally exciting, that the crowd didn't want to let her go when the song was over. It was truly a once-in-a-lifetime treat.

The bulk of the summer and fall of 1997 found LeAnn Rimes busy writing, touring, recording, and filming her first TV movie. The first new by-product of all this creative activity came in September of 1997, in the embodiment of her third album, "You Light Up My Life / Inspirational Songs." It was a dramatically different and highly successful career turn for her. Instead of singing songs about love and romance, all of the selections on her third album have a non-denominational overtone of religion, faith, and patriotism.

The album features several rock and pop classics from the past three decades, notably: Bette Midler's "The Rose," Paul Simon's "Bridge Over Trouble Water," and Debby Boone's "You Light Up My Life." She also sings two angel themed tunes: "Ten Thousand Angels Cried" and "On the Side Of Angels." However, it is Bill Mack's "Clinging To A Saving Hand" that is the album's stand out cut. Then there is the Diane Warren masterpiece of a song, "How Do I Live." Again, the album was produced by LeAnn's father, Wilbur Rimes.

THE "INSPIRATIONAL" ALBUM

The most critical aspect of the album was the inclusion of the ever-popular songs "God Bless America," "Amazing Grace" and the National Anthem—"The Star Spangled Banner." These songs marked a radical move for LeAnn, away from the more pop based repertoire of her previous pair of multi-"Platinum" albums.

What were the reasons for cutting such religious and/or patriotic songs amidst a hot career which—up until that point—was based solely on adult contemporary themes? Was it a way of countering the criticism she had received for singing songs like the older-than-her-years "My Baby" from the "Blue" album? Or was it her way of appealing to three different markets at once: Country, Pop, and Contemporary Christian?

According to Mike Curb, LeAnn's record company president, "It was originally their [the Rimeses'] idea to do an inspirational album. I think we [Curb Records] tried to position it so it could go into all three markets." (C)

It was however, Curb's idea for LeAnn to record the song "You Light Up My Life," so that the album wouldn't be all traditional spiritual songs, and would have a bit more of a contemporary light as well. It was 20 years ago that Curb himself released the original version of that song, as recorded by Debby Boone. It became the absolute zenith of Boone's popular recording career. How fitting that the torch should be passed to Miss Rimes.

Speaking of the concept and ultimate released version of the album, Mike Curb explains, "It started off more in the gospel direction and ended up a little more on the inspirational side." (C) Several critics really jumped on the startling career shift that this religious and patriotic album represented. One of the most scathing ones came in the "New York Daily News." Under the heading "LeAnn 'Light,'" writer Jim Farber went for the jugular vein when he announced, "Last year, 14-year-old LeAnn Rimes yodeled onto the scene with the grace, confidence and emotion of a new Patsy Cline. Who could have guessed that just one year later she'd come schlumping back with the corniness, greed and bad taste of a new Kathie Lee Gifford?" (CC) As bad as that may seem on the surface, fans don't care about reviews, so they were obviously unaffected by such press pronouncements.

When the album was released in September of 1997, it immediately hit Number One on the "Pop," "Country," AND "Contemporary Christian" charts in "Billboard" magazine. This made LeAnn the first country artist—male or female—to perform that exact task. Advisors might have called her "crazy" for tackling such flag-waving songs as the National Anthem or "God Bless America," but LeAnn couldn't have cared less. Apparently, she was crazy all right, crazy like a fox.

LIGHTS, CAMERAS, DRAMA

*E*ven the most beloved fairy tales have tragic occurrences, and LeAnn's tremendous trajectory from young hopeful to international singing star has taken its toll on her family. It was in the end of September and beginning of October 1997, when rumblings about Wilbur and Belinda Rimes' marriage ending first began to surface in the press. Having earned a reported $10 million dollars since the "Blue" album was released in July of 1996, the split of profits, the pending divorce settlement was suddenly big news.

Apparently, things had gotten so bad on the road, that LeAnn and family purchased another tour bus, so that her mother and her father could be in separate vehicles on the road. Finally, pressured into it, it was in October that LeAnn's hired publicity firm, Rogers & Cowan issued the following brief statement on the subject, stating: "Wilbur and Belinda are divorcing. LeAnn loves her mom and dad and supports them." (FF)

In the December 1997 issue of "Seventeen" magazine, LeAnn revealed that her mother decided that she would go home to the Dallas area for a bit of a rest, and let Wilbur look out for her. Reported LeAnn of mom Belinda, "She calls me all the time. I've been with them 24-7 [twenty four hours a day, seven days a week] forever, so it's kind of good to get away, but I also miss them when I do." (A)

Wilbur had to admit, "She's in a grownup world, and she's really advanced for her age. So maybe in that aspect she's grown-up a little too quickly, but I don't know if that's good or bad. We'll see." (L)

LeAnn had to admit at the time, "My success has changed our lives forever. I just want my parents to be happy, either together or alone...that is all I truly want." (EE) While the press pondered whether or not the Rimeses' split would become as nasty as that of child actor Macaulay Culkin's parents, it was business as usual for LeAnn. She had music to record, concerts to perform, movies to film, and interviews to give.

It is kind of ironic to see LeAnn's parents' marriage hit the rocks like this. The last time a teenager had such a million-selling streak on the record charts, Debbie Gibson in the 1980's, the exact same thing happened to her mom and dad. As soon as Debbie's career hit its zenith, her parents split up as well. In November of 1997, the tabloid newspapers in America were already reporting Wilbur Rimes' budding romance with 36-year-old Catherine Dickenson, who works for the company Brake Alert, in Minneapolis, Minnesota. That is the company which sells and services the tour busses LeAnn rides cross country in when she travels from concert venue to concert venue.

According to Belinda, "The divorce is affecting her. Kids don't want their parents to divorce. It's been hard on her and she's feeling the stress of it." (GG)

Of all of the accomplishments that LeAnn Rimes logged in 1997, two of the most significant ones included writing her own Christmas fable, "Holiday In Your Heart," and filming the movie version of the book for network television. It was an impressive, music-filled film, which proved a huge ratings success when it was first broadcast in America on ABC-TV, December 14, 1997. As evidenced by her acting job on this film, LeAnn was so refreshing and natural on camera, a fully developed acting career is clearly underway for her.

In fact, word had circulated so quickly throughout Hollywood as to how good she was as an actress, that before "Holiday In Your Heart" was even broadcast, movie studios were already phoning Wilbur Rimes, and offering LeAnn her own three-picture film deals. By the time December 1997 had rolled around, she had just scored another huge Number One on the country charts with the single

"How Do I Live," which had sold two million copies. "You Light Up My Life" was still on the charts, and "On The Side Of Angels" was in the Top 40, and still climbing. Suddenly, she was everywhere!

On December 4, 1997, LeAnn Rimes was seen promoting her movie, on TV's "The Tonight Show." Just to get into the Christmas mood, and set the scene for her film debut, she also sang a holiday song on the air. The excitement was already mounting for the public to see her movie.

The following Monday, December 8, LeAnn was one of the featured performers on the live telecast of "The 1997 Billboard Music Awards." Not only did she get to perform her hit "How Do I Live" at the MGM Grand Hotel in Las Vegas—on the same stage as The Spice Girls, Garth Brooks, and Aerosmith—but she also walked home with four of the top prizes. With the sales track record she had logged in the past year, it was no shock that she would win the "Country Album Of The Year" award for "Blue," AND the top "Country Singles Artist Of The Year." However, when it was announced that she had beat Alan Jackson, Deana Carter, AND George Strait to be named the "Country Artist Of The Year" it was quite an honor. As if those three honors weren't enough, at the crescendo of the evening—much to her surprise and amazement—she also won the top award as the "Entertainer Of The Year." All four of the nominees were women who had made a huge splash on the record charts in 1997: The Spice Girls, Jewel, Toni Braxton, and LeAnn Rimes. Accepting the award, LeAnn humbly thanked all of her fans, proclaiming, "You have made the past year, the best year of my life!" (II)

chapter six

LIGHTS,

CAMERAS,

DRAMA

"YOU HAVE MADE THE PAST YEAR, THE BEST YEAR OF MY LIFE!"

(LeAnn's message to her fans)

LIGHTS, CAMERAS, DRAMA

The following Sunday, December 14, "Holiday In Your Heart" had its premiere airing. In the film, LeAnn portrayed the fictional role of "LeAnn," a Nashville newcomer who is determined to launch her country singing career in Nashville. Along the way she befriends a has-been country singer from the past, by the name of Faith Shawn, played by Bernadette Peters. Dallas actress Carol Farabee is seen as fictional "LeAnn's" mother. To accommodate LeAnn's busy schedule, the film wasn't actually filmed in Nashville, Tennessee, but in Dallas, Texas. The entire movie was filmed in 18 days in 85 degree weather. In spite of the warm weather in Dallas, the story is set in ice cold Christmas-time Nashville, so the actors had to pretend that they were freezing in the cold weather, while they were in fact roasting in their winter coats.

According to LeAnn, she was totally bitten by the acting "bug," while filming this charming and modern Christmas fable. Although she was a bit nervous about her acting ability at first, after a couple of days she began to relax and really enjoy it. "Acting is hard work and a lot different from singing. It's not like anything I've ever done. People will see me in a completely different light," she claimed while amid production. (Q)

One of the biggest thrills she had was working with one of the most versatile actresses in Hollywood today, Bernadette Peters. "I've had so much fun with Bernadette," Rimes claims. "One of my favorite movies is 'Annie' and she was in that. And 'The Jerk.' It is really neat to get to work with her because I've watched her in so many films since I was a kid. She's a terrific lady and now we're good friends. I like that. To watch her is interesting. I'm a beginner, so to see someone who's been so successful for a long time in the acting field is perfect for me. I keep an eye on Bernadette and I learn from her." (Q)

Peters returned the compliment by stating, "LeAnn is very 'there' and focused in the dramatic scenes, and she's ready to have fun in the scenes you can have fun with. She's very professional and committed. I thought I might have to do something different working with someone who has never acted and who is 15 years old. I haven't had to do anything different." (Q)

LeAnn's book was adapted for the screen by noted screenplay writer Ellen Weston. According to her, "LeAnn is an amazing child. She takes the dialogue I've written and runs with it in a remarkable way. Actors train for years to get what she has naturally." (Q)

Several people who have suddenly gotten into acting on film, had been disillusioned by how difficult the "start and stop" schedule that filming a movie usually is produced on. But not Rimes. "I'm having the best time I've ever had in my life," LeAnn said amidst the the hectic filming. "I want to do more acting. It allows me to express my creativity in another way. I think it would be easier tackling a role where I wouldn't be playing me, where I would be someone else entirely. That's the kind of role I want to do in the future." (Q)

It had been one long whirlwind of a year for LeAnn Rimes. But, did she complain? Absolutely not. Instead she was able to exclaim, "1997 has been the best year yet for me!" (AA) And the excitement for her was only just beginning.

chapter seven

LIFE WITH LEANN

*I*t seems like the whole world is keeping busy speculating what life for LeAnn Rimes must be like from her perch at the absolute top of the country music world. Can she handle the pressure? Is she completely devastated by her parent's forthcoming divorce? Is she going to turn into a teenage hellion the way that Tanya Tucker admittedly did? Does she miss doing things that most girls her age take for granted? Is life on the road a nuisance? Or, through it all, is she having the time of her life?

Well, according to LeAnn herself, the answers to the above are: yes, no, no, no, no, and yes! In response to the first question: pressure? What pressure? She is simply doing what she always intended to do with her life. How many 15-year-olds can say that about their existences? LeAnn gleefully proclaims, "This is so much fun, I wouldn't trade it for anything." (M) With an attitude like that, what could possibly go wrong?

Well, her parents' upcoming divorce is not something that she would want to happen. However, she is also mature enough to realize that she wants both her mom and her dad to be happy with their lives, whether they are married to each other or not. She loves them both, and realizes that they both love her, so she isn't really losing anything by their separation.

Now that her mother isn't on the road with her and her dad all of the time, LeAnn feels no less close to either of them. Most teenagers LeAnn's age actually relish being out of their parents' watchful eye some of the time.

This all brings us up to the question about LeAnn following in Tanya Tucker's legendary "wild child" footsteps. That isn't about to happen. According to the "National Enquirer" (October 7, 1997), her father recently caught one of LeAnn's band members flirting with his daughter, and the young man was fired immediately. (EE) Addressing the question of dating, LeAnn herself explains, "My Dad's pretty open; my Mom's not. She freaks!" However, LeAnn is quick to admit, 'I'm not dating anyone, because I don't have time." (A)

With regard to her life on the road, in the last year and a half, LeAnn has become as at home on her tour bus, as she ever was in her bedroom in Dallas. Along with her on the road is her growing CD collection, a complete stock of videos, and an ever-growing wardrobe of clothes, for both on stage and for off.

One of the other reasons that she feels so comfortable on stage and on the road, is the fact that she has had the same core touring band all through her career. Several of them have become like family members to her, so there is nothing foreign about performing with them night after night. According to her, "I've known them all since I was six years old, so they're like big brothers and sisters to me. Even if they're not playing with me—like when I do awards shows—I have to have them on the road with me." (K) They have become a surrogate support system for Rimes, and they are extremely devoted to her.

"They're so much fun," LeAnn further proclaims. "We either work or play games or watch movies. That kind of stuff." (M)

There are moments when LeAnn does miss her privacy a bit. "I feel like I don't have a private life anymore. My private life is everyone else's. I'm sure all artists and stars in this business feel like that. I went to a lake the other day in a town of about 50 people, and it ended up in the newspaper. It's like, 'Okay, I can't go anywhere,'" (A) she explains.

She does admit that it can sometimes be a hassle to have to conceal her identity in dark glasses, and baggy clothes. LeAnn laughs, "I have a Nike shirt that says, 'I AM TIGER WOODS.' And, I love that shirt. I wear it everywhere I go. Because people come up and ask, 'Are you LeAnn Rimes?' And I say, 'No, can't you read my shirt? I'm Tiger Woods!'" (A)

Because she is on the road so much lately, does LeAnn have time for her hobbies anymore? "Not really anymore," she answers. "I mean, I've been pretty busy on the road, but In my free time I like to play softball, and I like cutting horses. Let's see. I like to go to movies and go shopping. Love to do that. I'm just a regular person like anyone else." (R)

Well, when you think about it, what could be a better dream for someone who likes to shop, than to be traveling across America from city to city? Just think of all those shopping malls you could go and visit! When asked recently where she enjoyed hunting for new bargains, she replied, "My favorite place to shop—I'd probably have to say The Limited and the Guess [Jeans] store." (R)

All of her life LeAnn has been in love with horseback riding. That is probably the one hobby she doesn't get much of a chance to do lately. "Well, I originally lived, where I grew up, in Mississippi—that's where I was born, in Jackson. I was around horses there, but when we moved up to Texas, I didn't have a place to ride them. So then I started back riding some horses again and about a year and a half ago [1994-1995] and I started 'cutting' and everything. I've been riding for about...a long time." (R)

For those who don't know what "cutting" is in equestrian—or "horse" terms, LeAnn explains, "It's where you're on a horse and you go into a herd of cattle and you cut out a cow, you know, you move them in front of the herd, and keep one cow in front and try to keep the cow from going back into the herd. Cutting is just a sport." (R)

If you were to spend the day hanging out with LeAnn Rimes, and you wanted to do some of the things that she likes the best, what would you be in store for? Well, as a reference guide, here are some of the things that she lists as her favorites:

LEANN'S FAVORITE COLOR:
BLUE (NATURALLY!!!)

LEANN'S FAVORITE FOODS:
PASTA, PIZZA, CHICKEN, STEAK, AND BACON BAKED POTATOES

LEANN'S FAVORITE RESTAURANT DISH:
*"CHICKEN PASTA—THERE'S A RESTAURANT IN DALLAS THAT MAKES IT AND I
JUST LOVE IT!" SHE PROCLAIMS. (R)*

LEANN'S FAVORITE FOOD HER MOTHER MAKES:
CHICKEN WITH SWISS CHEESE AND BREAD CRUMBS

LEANN'S FAVORITE SANDWICH:
GRILLED HAM AND CHEESE ON WHITE BREAD

LEANN'S FAVORITE DRINK:
COCA-COLA

LEANN'S FAVORITE DESSERT:
STRAWBERRY ICE CREAM SODA

LEANN'S FAVORITE MIDNIGHT SNACK:
CHEEZ-ITS CRACKERS

LEANN'S FAVORITE MALE SINGERS:
*BRYAN WHITE, ALAN JACKSON, BILLY DEAN, MICHAEL BOLTON, AND HANK
WILLIAMS SR.*

LEANN'S FAVORITE FEMALE SINGERS:
*PATSY CLINE, REBA McENTIRE, WYNONNA JUDD, BRANDY, CELINE DION,
BARBARA STREISAND, AND WHITNEY HOUSTON*

LEANN'S FAVORITE ROCK GUITARIST:
PRINCE

LEANN'S FAVORITE ROCK GROUP:
AEROSMITH

LEANN'S FAVORITE PASTIME:
SHOPPING

LEANN'S FAVORITE HOBBIES:
HORSEBACK RIDING, TENNIS, SWIMMING

LEANN'S FAVORITE CLOTHES:
T - SHIRT AND JEANS, CASUAL CLOTHES

LEANN'S FAVORITE SCHOOL SUBJECT:
MATHEMATICS

LEANN'S FAVORITE MOVIE:
"THE BODYGUARD"

LEANN'S FAVORITE TV SHOW:
"FRIENDS"

LEANN'S FAVORITE BOOK:
"DIARY OF ANNE FRANK"

In other words, at the age of 15, LeAnn Rimes has many of the same likes and dislikes as many girls her age. Is she sad about the fact that she will never attend her high school prom? According to her: not at all. She answers by asking how she could miss not having something that she has never had.

"I don't think I'm really giving up a lot," she says, "because I'm achieving a lot right now. I do have a different life, and I've grown up in an adult world. I don't have any friends my age. I don't mind that. I don't mind giving up the prom kind of thing and all that. I really don't think I'm missing out on anything 'cause this is what I want to do." (J)

The only difference between LeAnn and other girls her age, is the fact that she is in total control of her VERY HAPPENING career. She is phenomenally talented, she is destined to become a movie star as well as a singing star. And, she has earned over $10 million. Has she earned the right to be "blue?" Hardly. With all of these things going for her: Who needs the prom!?!

LEANN'S BRILLIANT FUTURE

A s 1997 ended, LeAnn was already in the recording studio working on her fourth album. At first, this one too was to have a theme to it. As it was originally planned, it was to contain only original songs that strongly reflected the way LeAnn herself felt about her life and her career. However, after she had such a huge success with the song "How Do I Live," which was written by mega hit-maker Diane Warren, she decided to stretch it out, and include other songwriters on the album as well. Although the concept changed a little bit, it is still expected to be deeply personal in content, and—if history repeats itself—it too will instantly hit the Number One slot on the record charts.

According to LeAnn, "I've been really involved in this album with the arranging, and I've been writing songs with my band. I wrote one called 'More Than Anyone Deserves,' and I have a song on there Bryan White wrote called 'When Am I Gonna Get Over You.' We have also cut three Diane Warren songs for this album." (V)

Diane Warren in the past has written hit songs for everyone in show business from Michael Bolton to Cher, and everyone in between. Interviewed amid the recording process of LeAnn's fourth album, Warren proclaimed, "Today was the most awesome, amazing day. I got to see LeAnn sing two of my songs, and she blew me away, as she always does." (V)

While most recording artists want to make certain that there is some continuity from album-to-album, in their performance and their voice, it is acknowledged that this is a bit impossible for LeAnn. Considering that the "Blue" album was recorded when she was 13, the "Unchained Melody" album was recorded when she was 11, and the "You Light Up My Life" album was recorded when she was 14 going on 15, her voice is still growing and developing. According to her father, "Her voice changes about every six months. By the time you finish one album, she's different again. Now the maturity is coming into it. Where she used to be this kid who could sing real high, now she can cover from the bottom to the top." (L) The way it has worked out for her, Number One album-to-Number One album, LeAnn's growing legion of devoted fans is following the development of her voice as she grows and matures.

Although she is still amidst her first 24 months as a nationally recognized singing star, she has been constantly gaining confidence. "When 'Blue' was first released, I was seen more as a novelty act, but I think that's blowing over now," she says. "Clearly it's not just a one-hit wonder thing. I want to be known as an artist and for my music, not just as a '15-year-old singing sensation.' I'm not going to be 15 forever; I don't want to be 25 and have people saying, 'Oh, she was better back then.'" (T)

Because she has appealed to such a wide range of music listeners, what audience is she going to aim her material at in the future? "What I wanna keep doing is keep my albums so there is traditional and contemporary country through everything, so there's a wide spectrum of music for everyone and for all age groups" she claims. (I) In other words: Why not go for it all?

When it comes down to role models in the country music business, who does LeAnn look up to the most? "If I had to model my career after anyone it would have to be Reba [McEntire]," Rimes says.

"She's made some great business decisions in her career to stay around for 20 years, and my biggest goal right now is to stay around for a long time." (D)

Watching McEntire go from being an aggressive and self-confident rodeo singer from Oklahoma, into a multimillion dollar one-woman industry, has been truly inspiring for LeAnn. The 15-year-old star is most fascinated in the way in which McEntire and her husband/manager have steered her career. "Reba has made some great business decisions," says LeAnn, "and she's stayed around for 29 years and hopefully I'll be able to do that." (P) Just as McEntire has gone from hit-making singer, to author, to movie star, Rimes has too.

Although LeAnn's father is her manager, and figuratively "behind the driving wheel," it is young Miss Rimes who is the navigator. If they make a turn in her career, it is only because she has deemed it to be so. "The smartest thing I've ever done for myself is take control of what I do," she proudly exclaims. "Hey, this is my life. Not just everyone else's to take a piece of. I've learned I need to please myself more than I need to please anyone else. If I can't make myself happy, there's no way I'm going to make anyone else happy. That, and don't take any crap off of anybody. The real world is hard; it's not what anybody thinks it is. What I'm doing is not all glitz and glamour. It's a job." (A) And, as all of Nashville looks on in awe, it is obviously a job well done.

The accolades she has received from the music-making elite of '90's Nashville: "I really love her to death, and realize that she's gonna be around for 30 or 40 years, you can count on it," predicts Vince Gill. "I think that there's so much attention being paid to the youth and I think that's good. Especially when they're as talented as she is. I don't care if she's 15 or 54. The fact is, she opens her mouth and she sings great. So it shouldn't matter." (W)

LeAnn's idol and friend, Wynonna Judd says of Rimes, "You don't hear voices like that anymore, voices that catch your ear in a few seconds." (O) Dolly Parton, who became a solo singing star who toured with a band comprised of her family members, "You have to rely on your own gut instincts and the family thing, and not lose your place and let ego or other people's flowery words pull you astray. LeAnn certainly has the gift." (P) And, Pam Tillis, exclaims, "What an incredible voice!" (HH)

In light of LeAnn's being named "Entertainer Of The Year" by "Billboard" magazine in December of 1997, the stakes have certainly heated up for her career. It is easy to see that there will be somewhat of a Rimes family tug-o-war over what she should be doing in 1998 and beyond. While her father, Wilbur, is pushing for her to "strike while the iron is hot;" it is her mother, Belinda, who is championing a bit of a slow-down. According to her, "She's entering her teenage years, and [the demands of a show business life] are not normal issues for someone her age to deal with. I worry about what lies ahead." (O)

Defining her specific role in her daughter's life right now, she proclaims, "My job right now, is to keep her head on straight, keep her honorable...She's a God-given child with God-given talent." (N)

Still, Belinda is bewildered by LeAnn's boundless energy and determination. "Some of the time, when I really feel tired and I'm thinking, 'Whew! Can I go on from here?' She gets on that stage, and the people start going crazy, and you think, 'She's having a good time!' What can you do? She's enjoying every minute of it. You'd be behind her 100 percent," she says supportively. (N)

Occasionally she laughingly ponders what would happen if the mother and daughter roles were reversed, by stating, "I wonder sometimes if when she has children of her own, will she do all that with them?" (N) Only time will tell on that matter.

"Truthfully," says LeAnn, "what's happened to me in this short period of time usually happens to an artist over three or four years. It's been a little overwhelming. I think I'm handling it OK; personally, I don't think I have changed at all. I think I still am the same person I've always been. Right now I can't walk around anywhere without someone noticing who I am or asking for an autograph, which I don't mind. I'm used to that now. I'm able to go out and perform all over the world and see fans—that's probably the best part for me,

even when I was just a local star around Texas. So, I'm just taking it day by day and enjoying it for what it is. I've wanted it for so long; I'm just trying to enjoy it. I know it sounds kind of funny, but I've been working hard for it since I was five. I might've started a little younger than most, but I've been working hard at it." (T)

Unlike most child stars in the past, LeAnn Rimes is in control of what is going on in her career, and she is not the product of some star-making machinery. "I'm very involved in the business part of my career. That's one thing I don't stay out of...I want to know what's going on. Because it's my life," she insists. (N) She set a goal, and put all of her time and her creative energy into attaining it. What kind of advice would she give to other kids with similar aspirations? "Just go for it!" LeAnn exclaims. "I mean, if it's something you love and something you want to do, just try your best and do what you can." (R) She certainly is living proof that anything is possible with the right attitude, the right amount of talent, and the right breaks.

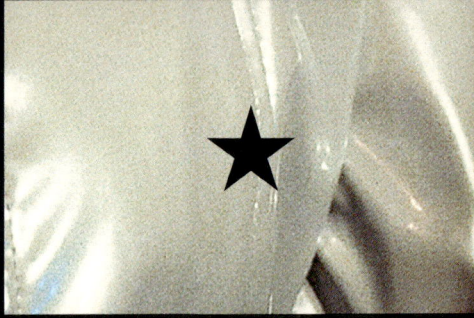

LEANN'S BRILLIANT FUTURE

She is very thankful for all of the opportunities that she has had in the last two years, and is quick to admit, "Most 15 year olds would give anything to be where I am. But I always tell them that if you want to get into this, you have to love it. It can get tiring. It's not all glamour and fortune. I'm working very hard now, basically, I have a job I have to do." (T)

Aside from her career, she has even toyed with the idea of college. "I'm going to finish my high school education. I think that I'm going to see where my career is at the time I'm getting ready to go to college and I'll probably go, but I just want to see where my career is at the time," she surmises. (R)

If she were to do that, what course of study would she like to major in? "I really love children, that's a big thing for me. So, I've always wanted to help children in any way, I think I'd like to major in Speech Pathology and help kids with speech problems." (R) Anyone who has seen her on television lately, will attest to the eloquent way in which she holds herself, and expresses herself. If she were to set her mind to helping others as a serious goal, apparently, there would be absolutely no stopping her!

With the riches that LeAnn has amassed, as 1998 begins, she is amidst the construction of a new 3,700 square foot home for her family, in Nashville, Tennessee. Predicted her mother, "Next year [1998], we're going to slow down. LeAnn is not going to be on the road all the time. She's going to act like a kid and have a more normal life. Her success happened too fast. We were on the road every day and it was taking a toll on all of us." (GG)

Well, like most teenage girls, LeAnn Rimes has some slightly different ideas on this subject, than her mother does. It is hard to imagine, in light of all the wonderful things that have happened to her in the past two years, that she will be content to sit still in a gorgeous house in Nashville, just doing her homework, and perusing through college brochures.

Like the conviction that she puts into singing her brilliant hit single, "How Do I Live," how could she possibly live far from the spotlight, after tasting the kind of success that she has experienced? In the meantime, LeAnn's growing legion of fans, anxiously await the next project from her, whether it is her latest album, her newest concert tour, her next movie, or whatever else she becomes involved in.

With an already well-established singing career—based on a phenomenal voice, and a lot of determination—LeAnn has become a major country singing star, while still looking forward to her 16th birthday. She has the look, the sound, the right attitude, and now—the star stature she has longed for. What she does with the brass ring of success that she is so soundly grasping in her hands, is entirely in her control. She is obviously at the beginning of a long and successful career, and much to the public's delight, there is much, much more to come from the brilliant LeAnn Rimes.

"UNCHAINED MELODY/
The Early Years" (Curb Records / 1997)

1. **"I Want To Be A Cowboy's Sweetheart"** (Patsy Montana)

2. **"I Will Always Love You"** (Dolly Parton)

3. **"Blue Moon Of Kentucky"** (Bill Monroe)

4. **"River Of Love"** (Vip Vipperman, Buddy Blackmon)

5. **"The Rest Is History"** (Clay Blaker, Karen Staley)

5. **"Broken Wing"** (David Nowlen)

7. **"Yesterday"** (John Lennon, Paul McCartney)

8. **"Sure Thing"** (Joyce Harrison)

9. **"Share My Love"** (LeAnn Rimes, Blake Vickers)

10. **"Unchained Melody"** (Alex North, Hy Zares)

★

"YOU LIGHT UP MY LIFE / Inspirational Songs"
(Curb Records / 1997)

1. "You Light Up My Life" (Joe Brooks)
2. "The Rose" (Amanda McBroom)
3. "Bridge Over Troubled Water" (Paul Simon)
4. "I Believe" (J. Shirl, A. Stillman, E. Drake, I. Graham)
5. "Ten Thousand Angels Cried" (David Patillo)
6. "Clinging To A Saving Hand" (Bill Mack)
7. "On The Side Of Angels" (Gary Burr, Gerry House)
8. "I Know Who Holds Tomorrow" (Ira F. Stanphill)
9. "God Bless America" (Irving Berlin)
10. "How Do I Live" (extended mix) (Diane Warren)
11. "Amazing Grace" (Traditional)
12. "National Anthem" / "Star Spangled Banner"

"SITTIN' ON TOP OF THE WORLD"
(Curb Records / 1998)

1. "Commitment" (Tony Colton, Tony Marty, Bobby Wood)
2. "Looking Through Your Eyes" (Deborah Allen, Rafe Van Hoy)
3. "Feels Like Home" (Diane Warren)
4. "Surrender" (Robin Lee Bruce, Christi Dannemiller, Jamie O'Neal)
5. "These Arms of Mine" (Jeff Tweel, Gail Thompson)
5. "Nothin' New Under The Moon " (Rick Bowles, Tom Shapiro, Josh Leo)
7. "When Am I Gonna Get Over You" (Bryan White, John Tiro)
8. "Rock Me" (Deborah Allen, Rafe Van Hoy)
9. "More Than Anyone Deserves" (LeAnn Rimes, Ron Grimes)
10. "Insensitive" (Anne Loree)
11. "All the Lovin' and the Hurtin'" (Deborah Allen, Rafe Van Hoy)
12. "Sittin' On Top Of The World" (Amanda Marshall)
13. "The Heart Never Forgets" (Jerry Williams, Frank L. Myers, Gary Baker)
14. "Purple Rain" (Prince)

★

BIBLIOGRAPHY

(A) "Seventeen," magazine, December 1997, "Get On The Bus With LeAnn Rimes" by Lauren Oliver

(B) "Country Weekly," magazine, July 16, 1996, "Country's New Princess: Teen Phenom LeAnn Rimes" by Larry Holden

(C) "Chicago Tribune," newspaper, October 5, 1997, "Rimes Crossover Album Is A Marketing Inspiration," by Jack Hurst

(D) "New York Times," newspaper, August 25, 1996, "Big Voice, Big Dreams and All of 13," by Bruce Feiler

(E) "Entertainment Weekly," magazine, December 20, 1996, "My Year That Was: LeAnn Rimes, John Leguizamo, Matthew Broderick, & Noah Wyle"

(F) "Washington Post," newspaper, June 22, 1996, "Crazy, Crazy for Her," by Sue Anne Pressley

(G) "Houston Chronicle," newspaper, May 31, 1996, "At 13, gifted LeAnn Rimes Makes Heads Turn And Stirs Up Airwaves," by Rick Mitchell

(H) "Ft. Worth Star Telegram," newspaper, June 22, 1996, "The New Patsy Cline," by Shirley Jinkins

(I) "Texas Monthly," magazine, October 1996, "The Kids Are Alright: LeAnn Rimes," by John Morthland

(J) "Los Angeles Times," newspaper, July 27, 1996, "What's She Got To Be Blue About?," by Richard Cromelin

(K) "Rolling Stone," magazine, June 24, 1997, "Raves: LeAnn Rimes," compiled by Anthony Bozza

(L) "Time," magazine, March 10, 1997, "Blue Chip Kid," by Christopher John Farley

(M) "Los Angeles Daily News," newspaper, August 8, 1996, "The Age Of Rimes," by Fred Shuster

(N) "USA Weekend," magazine, September 27-29, 1996, "Country's Teen Of Hearts," by Jennifer Mendelsohn

(O) "People," magazine, September 2, 1996, "Rimes With Talent," by Calvin Baker and Bob Stewart

(P) "TV Guide," magazine, September 28, 1996, "Nashville's Teen Queen," by Chet Flippo

(Q) "Country Weekly," magazine, November 11, 1997, "LeAnn's A Natural As She Heads In A New Direction / Behind The Scenes Of her Movie Debut," by Larry Holden

(R) Interview with LeAnn Rimes by Marie Morreale, August 20, 1996, transcript

(S) "LeAnn Rimes, A Biography," press biography, Rogers & Cowan

(T) "Country Song RoundUp," magazine, October 1997, "LeAnn Rimes, The Sky's The Limit," by Gary Graff

(U) "Atlanta Journal-Constitution," newspaper, June 15, 1996, "Living Out Of The Blue," by Miriam Longino

(V) "Billboard," magazine, November 28, 1997, "Curb's Rimes A Country Music Conqueror / Chart-Topping Teen's Star Continues To Rise," by Deborah Evans Price

(W) "Tucson Citizen," newspaper, October 24, 1996, "Miss Rimes and You'll Be Blue," by A.J. Flick

(X) "Wall Street Journal," newspaper, August 28, 1996, "Singin' An Oldie, She's Lookin' Like A Star," by Louise Lee

(Y) "USA Today," newspaper, June 11, 1996, "LeAnn Rimes Turns Nashville On Its Ear," by David Zimmerman

(Z) "Tucson Citizen," newspaper, November 1, 1996, "Alan Jackson Is All Cowboy at Halloween Performance," by A.J. Flick

(AA) "E! Entertainers '97." TV special, E! Entertainment Network, December 6, 1997

(BB) Associated Press News Service, April 23, 1997, "LeAnn Rimes Wins Two Country Music Awards"

(CC) "New York Daily News," newspaper, October 26, 1997, "LeAnn 'Light,'" by Jim Farber

(DD) "Star," newsmagazine, April 29, 1997, "Heartache For Teen Sensation LeAnn Rimes / She Misses TV Show As Parents Fight Over Her Career," by Roger Hitts

(EE) "National Enquirer," newsmagazine, October 7, 1997, "LeAnn Rimes' Shocker! Parents Are Divorcing," by Steve Herz, with Bennet Bolton and Chris Wessling

(FF) "Star," newsmagazine, October 19, 1997, "LeAnn Rimes In Bitter $10M Tug-Of-Love," by Roger Hitts

(GG) "Globe," newsmagazine, November 25, 1997, "LeAnn Rimes' Secret Agony," by Rod Gibson & Ken Harrell

(HH) "People," magazine, December 30, 1996 - January 6, 1997, "The 25 Most Intriguing People Of The Year"

(II) "The 1997 Billboard Music Awards," TV telecast, December 8, 1997, Fox Broadcasting Network

About the Author
MARK BEGO

Mark Bego is the author of several best-selling books on rock & roll and show business. With 32 books published and over 8 million books in print, he is acknowledged as the best-selling biographer in the rock and pop music field. His biographies have included the life stories of some of the biggest stars of ROCK (Elvis Presley, Michael Jackson, Madonna, Bonnie Raitt, The Doobie Brothers, Three Dog Night), SOUL (Aretha Franklin, The Supremes, Martha Reeves & The Vandellas, Whitney Houston), POP (Cher, The Monkees, Bette Midler, Sade, Barry Manilow), and COUNTRY (Patsy Cline, Alan Jackson, George Strait, LeAnn Rimes).

"The Tucson Citizen" recently featured Bego on the cover of its entertainment section, with regard to his transition from rock to country.   In the article, music writer A.J. Flick declared, "Rock 'n' Roll's biggest selling biographer has gone country...Mark Bego is tops in rock 'n' roll and pop biographies according to 'Publisher's Weekly'...Bego, who has written for fan magazines, uses an objective voice in his biographies...(he) understands the attraction of country music."

His biography of Michael Jackson—"Michael!" (1984)—spent six weeks on "The New York Times" Bestseller list, and the book he wrote with Motown star Martha Reeves—"Dancing In The Street: Confessions Of A Motown Diva" (1994)—spent five weeks on "The Chicago Tribune" bestseller list. Mark's other books for St. Martin's Press are: "Julian Lennon!" (1986), "The Best of 'Modern Screen'" (1986), "The Linda Gray Story" (1988), and "Aretha Franklin: Queen Of Soul" (1989) .